The Love Languages of Food

Written by

Chef Terrell Manning

The Love Languages of Food

Copyright © Terrell Manning, 2020

Cover image: © Terrell Manning

ISBN-13: 978-0-578-76333- 0

Publisher's Note

Printed and bound in the United States of America. All rights reserved. No part of this book may be reproduced or transmitted in any form or by any means, electronic or mechanical, including photocopying, recording, or by any information storage and retrieval system except by a reviewer who may quote brief passages in a review to be printed in a magazine, newspaper, or on the Web without permission in writing from **Terrell Manning**.

Although the author and publisher have made every effort to ensure the accuracy and completeness of information contained in this book, we assume no responsibility for errors, inaccuracies, omissions, or any inconsistency herein. The advice and strategies contained herein may not be suitable for your situation. You should consult with a professional where appropriate. Neither the publisher nor the author shall be liable for damages arising from here.

Dedication

The Love Languages of Food is dedicated to my father, Kevin Paul Manning, the most intellectual and brilliant man I have ever met.

The reason that there is a Chef Terrell Manning is because of my father. I vividly remember the conversation we had on the day of his passing. I was at a time in my life where I was unsure of my career choice, my abilities, and how successful I would be. My father sat me down and talked to me about the importance of following things you're passionate about while remaining even-keeled and methodical.

I relied heavily on my father's guidance and mentorship as I grew into the early stages of adulthood. Suddenly, I was at a crossroads about which culinary path I should pursue and truly had no answers for my own questions. I decided I wasn't going to make the decision; I would simply let my father decide which path would be best for me, and I would pursue that course of action.

When I brought my dilemma to my father, I was very confused by his response. He said that he didn't have an answer for me. That it was something he couldn't decide for me. Me being utterly shocked by his response, I began to delve into his reasoning and ask why he was suddenly drawing a blank. Understand my father was the smartest and wisest person I've ever been around; he somehow almost always made the perfect decisions and always had all of the answers.

He began telling me that this situation was something that I would have to figure out with my own wit, knowledge, and pure emotions. He continued by saying how he wouldn't always be around to help me with decisions and that it was time for me to start making decisions as a man and living with the rewards and or the consequences.

To my pops, from your boy.

The Love Languages of Food

Table of Contents

Dedication   2

Introduction   6

Love Language 1   8
- *Family Interactions*   8
- *Gramma's Pound Cake Recipe*   15

Love Language 2   17
- *Creativity & Curation*   17
- *Ma's Baked Mac & Cheese Recipe*   22

Love Language 3   24
- *Passion of Craftsmanship*   24
- *Chef Manning's Italian Table Loaf Bread*   29

Love Language 4   32
- *Respect*   32
- *Chef Manning's Orange Chicken*   40

The Love Languages of Food

Love Language 5   43

Cuisine & Culture   *43*

Chef Manning's Creole Jambalaya   *48*

Love Language 6   51

Validation & Confirmation   *51*

Chef Manning's Bread Pudding & Rum Sauce   *57*

Love Language 7   60

Friendship & Camaraderie   *60*

Chef Manning's Butter Cookies Recipe   *64*

About Chef Manning   67

Introduction

The Love Languages of Food is based on what I have experienced in my culinary journey and deemed to be the essential characteristics of any chef, home cook, foodie, or someone who flat out loves food.

At least one of these characteristics exist in every one of us. This book will help you determine what culinary love languages you possess within yourself and how to exploit those love languages to your advantage and enjoy food on a whole new level you never thought possible.

We love the culinary art form because of the craftsmanship that is required and the dedication that is committed to every dish that is curated. With this book, you will be able to sink your mind into the very depths of the level of hard work and skill required to create this form of art we know as food.

The Love Languages of Food

Love Language 1
Family Interactions

This love language resonates with most culinarians, whether at home or in a professional kitchen. We have something that brings us back to a time when someone close to us made us food. It brings about a distinct memory that allows us to briefly be present in that moment. We remember the way the food smelled, the way it tasted, and of course, the way it made us feel.

"Never put a cap on your potential!"

-My Father

As a little boy, I would stand on my tippy toes, barely overlooking our wooden dining room table, as I watched my grandmother prep to family dinner. She always had everything neatly placed and in order. My grandmother is very OCD when it comes to meal preparation. Once she arranged all of the ingredients out on the table, you just knew something magical was about to happen in the kitchen. She definitely had a system for how she made magic happen with food.

As I looked on, my curiosity and interest continuously increased. I wanted to be part of the process… I wanted to cook. My mother was always afraid of me being in the kitchen. I'm not sure exactly what she was scared of. It could have been she was concerned with the possible spills and the mess, or maybe it was the fear of me near a hot stove and sharp objects. However, my grandmother was not concerned at all!

Known as Miss or Pastor Mary Boyd to others and "Gramma" to me, she was the one who nurtured my cooking skills. Not only is she my culinary coach, but she is also my spiritual rock. She is fearless, beautiful, energetic, and possesses a work ethic that is legendary in my eyes.

She and my father's work ethic set the tone for my inner drive and work ethic. My father had what I called the "lunch pail and hard hat mentality." He was a hardworking man. He never called off sick. He showed up to work every day and gave one hundred percent. Now that I'm a father, I can admit that I see a lot of my father in myself when I am in "daddy mode." There are things that I do and say with my daughter that my father did and said to me.

My father was an honest man. He always kept his word. He raised me to be an ambitious, respectable man and to always be true about my thoughts and feelings. My father was big on accepting and owning up to responsibility, mistakes, winning seasons, losing seasons, earning potential, and accomplishments. Some of the best advice I have ever received came from the man who I called Pops.

Pops once told me to, "Never put a cap on your potential; it will cost you millions." It just so happens that he uttered these words to me the day of his unexpected passing. And that is just one of many of my father's words of wisdom.

He also said, "You will never max out on the amount of money and success you can earn if you follow your passion and do what you love." He always encouraged me to go after my dreams and do whatever I had a passion for. His only request was that I do it, do it well, and stick with it.

As I began my cooking career, I would come home from work wanting to cook even more and try out new recipes and creations, and let's just say I had some flops. My father was definitely a foodie and didn't mind trying new foods or creations. Pops tried any and everything I put in front of him. There were some dishes he had never heard of or experienced. Regardless, that never stopped my father. I could always count on his honesty and constructive criticism. That was how he showed support, and it made me a much better cook.

The Love Languages of Food

I appreciate that about my father still today. My father wasn't a man of the kitchen, but I could always count on him making his famous grilled cheese sandwiches every Sunday morning before we headed out for church. As I look back on my culinary journey, I am filled with joy! I had a supportive family, who believed in me, believed in my talent, and believed in my passion. I was never told that I could not do anything. I have always had free range to test the waters of my interest, even as a young boy fascinated with cooking. I wanted to learn everything there was to know, and my Gramma supported my urge.

My Gramma designed my first apron out of what I thought was pale green plastic. In fact, we had matching aprons. She had an adult version of mine. The truth is my apron did not start as an apron. It was created to protect my Gramma's car from my afterschool snacks and spills. Gramma was very particular when it came to her car. Her OCD was real.

At the tender age of seven, I had a lot of passion and interest in cooking. I was ready to put my pale green apron on and cook. It was my grandmother who picked up on my interest and decided to nurture my optimism. She knew I wanted to be more involved in preparing and cooking meals, and she chose to go with it. From that moment on, my quest to be a chef was born.

The Love Languages of Food

Studies have shown that spending time in the kitchen with children helps them learn basic math concepts, boosts their self-confidence, and builds language skills. I was learning all of that and then some. No one would believe that a little boy, who watched on as his grandmother and mother prepared meals could develop a love language of his own when it came to food... But I did!

During my first cooking experience, I remember reaching to grab an old wooden spoon that once belonged to my great grandmother to help my Gramma stir a pot of collard greens. This sparked more interest in making food from start to finish. My Gramma agreed to give me a few lessons to get me going.

The first lesson was scrambled eggs. My Gramma got me up bright and early and already had everything laid out that we would need. As I stood on my tippy toes and attempted to crack my first egg, I was unsuccessful. After several attempts, I finally did it. Not only did I successfully crack my first egg, but all of it also made it into the bowl. I was ecstatic! I had prepared my first scrambled egg!

And with my own two hands. Once I tasted them, I was hooked and ready to learn more.

We didn't just stop at scrambled eggs. I learned various ways to prepare eggs. I mean, who knew there were so many ways that one could prepare an egg. All the different textures, smells, and tastes from using various ingredients provided each egg recipe with its own unique flavor and taste.

Next up on Gramma's list was pancakes. But instead of us using the four-inch skillet, Gramma brought out the "big boy" griddle. I had graduated to a larger cooking surface.

As I read the instructions on the box, I knew exactly what ingredients were needed. The ingredients were fairly simple and basic, but my grandmother always added her own special touches, and adding those special touches is what she passed down to me. As I mixed all the ingredients into the bowl, I noticed how the batter went from white to a creamy brown color. Although my wrist was a little fatigued, I was ready for the pancake experience.

As I whisked the pancake batter, Gramma came over and corrected my technique. She said, "Baby, you're doing it wrong." She removed the whisk from my hand, grabbed the bowl, and began to whisk vigorously. Of course, she was ten times faster with it than I was.

Gramma had the whisking motion down to a science.

Next, we oiled down the "big boy" griddle. We used a 2-oz ladle spoon to scoop the batter. As expected, my first two weren't that great. When it came time for me to flip them, they splattered all over the griddle. But my grandmother stepped right in. She shared with me the importance of cooking and timing.

Each pancake needed at least four minutes on each side before flipping. I also discovered that the small bubbles that popped up on the pancakes' uncooked side were a sign that it was time for the pancakes to be flipped on the other side. Needless to say, my second batch was perfect! It was as if my Gramma had made them herself.

The Love Languages of Food

Gramma's Pound Cake Recipe
Inspired by *Love Language 1*

If *Love Language 1* had a specific recipe, it would be my Gramma's pound cake. When Gramma makes her pound cake, family and friends come out of nowhere to get a slice or a sliver depending on how close they are to Gramma's heart. The only tweaking I've done is added an extra half teaspoon of rum flavoring for my lush friends.

The Elements
1 lb of butter, softened
1 lb confectioners' sugar
6 eggs
1 teaspoon of rum flavor
½ teaspoon of lemon flavor
½ teaspoon of vanilla flavor
3 cups of cake flour, sifted

Take Action
1. Whip butter and then fold in sugar.
2. Once combined, add in all flavors.
3. Add in two eggs with one cup of sifted flour.
4. While mixer is on low setting, add in two more eggs and one more cup of flour.
5. Once mixed, add in remaining eggs.
6. Once eggs are mixed, add in remaining flour.
7. Mix all together.
8. Preheat oven to 350°F and bake for 55 minutes.
9. Place a small aluminum pan on a lower rack in the oven with an inch and a half of water to ensure moisture.

Love Language 2
Creativity & Curation

"Creativity is something that every foodie or chef has in them. It comes from sheer curiosity and the desire to make something great(er). You'll often find this love language in very innovative leaders. Regardless of the possible outcome, this love language depicts those who pay close attention to detail and always have a great idea about food."

-**Chef Terrell Manning**

That is NOT how we make it. If only I had a dollar for every time I heard that... Around the age of ten years old, I knew I was ready to take a shot at preparing my mother's (Ma) famous spaghetti. Ma's spaghetti is one of my absolute favorites. The combination of her grated onions, fresh garlic, basil, parsley, and ground beef combined with pork sausage is simply amazing! Now Ma is not as open-minded as I am when it comes to food. She is very old school and set in her ways when it comes to food. If it's not her way, it's not the right way.

As I watched her prepare, she instructed me to take notes, but me being who I am, I passed on the notes and decided to take mental notes instead. Besides, my Gramma had already taught me early on about the importance of being creative and adding a bit of yourself and your personality when cooking. My mom has made her meals a certain way for over thirty years, and whenever I drifted from her recipe, even if I just added a little of something new, "That's not the way I taught you," is what I would hear.

My mother and I have a very special love language regarding what's right and what's wrong when it comes to cooking. We are constantly bumping heads, especially when I veer away from what she considers to be the "original" way to prepare a meal. That translates to, "That's not the way I taught you!" Here's a quick example so that you can see that I am not exaggerating.

One day I prepared a pot of kale greens, and because my mother does not make hers with the stems… Yep, you guessed it. I did it wrong. It is not the way she taught me! Personally, I prefer to rough chop the stems and mix them in. The stems add great texture. They are friggin' delicious and should not be discarded. On the other hand, my mother wants them cut off and tossed in the trash.

Here's another prime example of our love language. When I prepared short ribs for dinner at home, I added a little tomato paste for flavor and coloring. Adding tomato paste makes for a more robust flavor and color and thickens the short ribs' drippings to make a really delicious sauce. And when my mom saw it, what do you think she said? "That's not my recipe!" But this time, I reminded her that I was the one who gave her the recipe for the short ribs.

True enough, in my original recipe, it doesn't consist of tomato paste, but at the last minute, I decided to add more flavor. It wasn't even her recipe. My mother and I always seem to be in a tug-of-war about food. However, after my Gramma decided I was going to learn how to cook, my mother stepped up to the plate and offered to teach me more of the intricate lessons of cooking.

One of my most memorable moments is when that ten-year old boy who watched, learned, and took mental notes of his mother cooking one of his favorite dishes grew as a chef and decided to tackle his mom's spaghetti. I was no longer the ten-year-old boy anymore; I was a bonafide chef and wanted to go back and make the meals I grew up enjoying.

Not only did I cook and perfect that very dish, the satisfying part came when Ma said that the spaghetti I made tasted exactly like hers. That brought out the ten-year-old boy in me and made me so happy!

To have the approval of my toughest critic was an awesome accomplishment. I don't believe she would have ever told me if mine was better than hers, so I took my compliment and moved on.

Every holiday, our family tradition was to have my dad barbecue for hours on end. I can remember my mom getting up early in the morning to season the meat and prepare all the side dishes and sauces, while my dad was outside on the grill.

I would begin my day assisting my mother in the kitchen. When I was done, I would go outside and spend the remaining parts of the day learning from my father about the proper temperatures for certain types of meat, when to turn the items on the grill but most importantly I learned how to protect the integrity of flavor and texture while grilling. After hours of grilling, my dad and I would go inside smelling like charcoal and a smokehouse. Finally, we could clean up and sit down with the rest of the family to eat a hard-earned family dinner.

My parents were married for over thirty years - both from the Southside of Chicago. I grew up watching my dad take my mom out on date night to her favorite restaurants. Food has always been a part of my family's love language. It was my mom who sparked my motivation to start cooking professionally in the first place. She inspired me to take my talent seriously and make a career out of it.

Ma is truly my backbone! She has an entrepreneurial mindset and knows how to capitalize on things and has continually encouraged me to capitalize on my ability to cook. She's extremely intelligent, and she puts a lot of herself in everything that she does, just like I do when I'm in the kitchen.

I inherited her creativity and ambition and simply applied it to food. She's an incredible woman, mother, daughter, and grandmother to my daughter. Now, if I could only learn to stay on course and stick to the recipes the way she taught me… Unfortunately, that's a promise I can't keep!

Ma's Baked Mac & Cheese Recipe
Inspired by *Love Language 2*

As you saw in Love Language 2, Ma and I have an interestingly good time in the kitchen with each other. This is probably my second favorite dish of my mother's behind the Spaghetti Bolognese. Ma's Mac & Cheese is so very cheesy and delicious inside and out, and of course, it's slow-baked.

The Elements

1 box of elbow macaroni

2 eggs

1 ½ cups of Sharp Cheddar cheese, freshly grated

1 cup of heavy whipping cream

3 teaspoons of sugar

2 tablespoon of butter, softened

1 tablespoon of seasoned salt

1 tablespoon of pepper

2 teaspoons of cayenne pepper

1 teaspoon of Louisiana Hot Sauce

Take Action

1. Pour box of elbow noodles into salted boiling water.
2. While pasta is cooking, whisk together cream, sugar, shredded cheese, and eggs on medium-low heat.
3. Add in all seasonings and hot sauce.
4. Once pasta has cooked and is slightly al dente, drain from the hot water, and toss macaroni with softened butter and combine with the mixture.
5. Whisk together.
6. Set oven to 350°F and cook for 25 minutes.

Love Language 3
Passion of Craftsmanship

Have you ever met a person that loves their journey and loves to share little known facts about their craft? Those are typically people who are sincerely passionate about what they do. Finding someone with this type of passion for food is like finding a diamond in the rough. They are rare and hard to find.

This love language has a small dosage of all of the other love languages compiled into one. When someone is cooking for you that is truly passionate about food, you can feel it in every bite. You can tell by the thoughtfulness of the plating, the depth of conversation when they talk about the dish, and the enthusiasm that they portray when they are preparing it.

"100% Passion & 100% Enthusiasm."

-Chef Terrell Manning

Working in a four-diamond resort was a dream that became my reality at the age of eighteen. At that time, my cooking experience was limited to my kitchen at home. That was my professional cooking space since the age of seven. I remember asking myself, "What are you doing here?" But I knew I already had the answer... I wanted to be there! I needed to be there! And most importantly, it was my passion.

I can recall my very first week. I had a notebook filled with recipes of dishes I never dreamed of making, ingredients I've never heard of, and instructions on developing mastery for a skill I was just beginning to learn. I was a sponge! I was soaking it all up!

The beautiful, perfectly equipped professional kitchen, the well-seasoned chefs, the high-quality products we received. Everything was perfect! There was much to learn, but I was ready and excited for the challenge. One of the first things that I noticed about my new world was that everyone moved differently. The language was different. Everything about the experience captured my interest in a way that is still hard to explain. It was as if everyone was somehow in a well-rehearsed orchestra. All of the movements were harmonious and graceful.

It was an environment that I waited my entire life to be a part of, but my first week was brutal. The chef cursed me out at least three times. He constantly corrected and scolded me for not getting certain things right(just like you see on TV). But that didn't bother me. My stern upbringing had forced me to be tough as nails and prepared me for days such as these.

I wasn't raised to be sensitive; I wasn't raised to give up or to quit. I understood that I had a skill to learn, and I knew I had to learn faster than normal. I was not going to be the weak link on my team. By the end of week one, I still could not tell you what an airline chicken breast was. It's actually known as "stalter" chicken—a breast of chicken with the drumette still attached.

I was constantly learning new things. My notebook was filled with new jargon and meanings. I loved the new love language. I was becoming attached to my newfound love language. My love and passion for food had reached a new high. By week two, I was still feeling a little out of place but not as much as the previous week. I spent hours dicing onions and peeling potatoes. I had become so good that I could peel an entire bag of potatoes in eighteen minutes or less.

Every day I arrived at work feeling as if I was in a movie. The experience was way more than I could have ever expected. All-day, I would hear the sounds of banging pots, pans, meat braising, and chefs cracking jokes on each other, all while others moved backwards and forward at rapid speeds all around me. By the end of each day, I would go home tired with blood-red eyes from the onions, and calluses on my hands from the cheap knife I was using. But I loved every minute of it.

I knew if I worked really hard and paid close attention, I would learn everything I needed to know. I walked in as an eighteen-year-old boy with a passion for cooking. I knew nothing about the industry like I do now, but I was determined and committed to my dream. I knew that I would emerge as a chef at the completion of my experience.

I remember being so curious about everything. I even wanted to know everyone else's purpose for wanting to be in the industry. I knew what drove me, but I wanted to know why they were there. Did they have the same commitment and passion that I had, or was it just a job to them?

As I asked more questions about everyone's journey, I realized that for most of my other chefs, they were promoted or pushed into the industry. Very few of them actually sought out this career or were following their passion. Then I had a thought. If they had the skills, knowledge, and understanding of all the essential functions, then they had little passion and enthusiasm. I realized I had one thing that no one else in that kitchen possessed - passion! I showed up every day with a gogetter mentality and used every single part of my day as motivation! No one had to push me or talk me into being there and being present.

I realized that if I kept developing my skill and improving my talent with 100% passion and 100% enthusiasm, my potential would be limitless. I applied everything I learned from that experience to my everyday cooking style and allowed it to set the tone for my quest to be a chef.

Chef Manning's Italian Table Loaf Bread
Inspired by *Love Language 3*

If you ever want to test out your culinary patience, whip up a couple of loaves of bread. The dough has to be kneaded properly. It takes multiple cycles of resting in a somewhat warm environment. This will test your attention to detail and your overall craftsmanship in the kitchen, which is why it pairs best with *Love Language 3*.

I originally wrote this recipe for a 5-course wine dinner. It was my take on Avocado on Toast with Lobster, which I like to call Lobstercado on Toast. It came out extremely well and paired perfectly with a 2017 Sauvignon Blanc.

The Elements

7 cups of bread flour

3 cups of water

2 tablespoons of instant yeast

3 teaspoons of salt

2 tablespoons of EVOO

1 tablespoon of sugar

10 tablespoons of dried oregano

10 tablespoons of thyme

10 tablespoons of parsley

10 tablespoons of basil

Take Action

1. Add yeast to water mix thoroughly until yeast dissolves.
2. Then add all flour to yeast and water mixture.
3. Sprinkle in salt and herbs.
4. Add oil last and mix thoroughly.
5. Hand knead dough for 8 minutes.
6. Let rest for 3 minutes.
7. After rested, sprinkle all of dough with flour and shape dough into a ball by folding the dough.

8. After ball is formed, sprinkle more flour on top, sit in a bowl with plastic wrap over the top, and sit for an hour.
9. After the dough has risen for an hour, take dough out of the bowl carefully and cut the dough in half evenly.
10. After separated pre-shape dough into a ball by folding in halves.
11. Let each half rest for 15 minutes.
12. After 15 minutes, flour the surface and press the dough down. Fold dough in a triangle shape to start forming for a loaf pan.
13. Once finished, roll the dough like a cigar to form. Crease the bottom seam of the dough and coat with flour.
14. Once in the loaf pan, let it rise for 1 hour.
15. Preheat oven to 400°F and bake for 35-40 minutes.
16. Poke with a toothpick to ensure the bread is baked thoroughly.
17. Let rest for at least 25-30 minutes.

Love Language 4
Respect

"Respect for the guests, respect for the quality of ingredients, and respect for the craft. This is definitely the most important love language to have. Having respect for what you put on a plate and knowing the backstory about your ingredients are essential. Ingredients are delicacies and should be treated as such. Using the freshest and most natural ingredients possible elevates the quality, the flavor, and even the presentation of the dish. Learning about the region of each ingredient and their prime seasons can also elevate your palate and your appreciation for the food that you are cooking and or eating."

-Chef Terrell Manning

After learning the industry for a bit, I decided to learn other cuisines and some other cultures. My next venture was learning Asian cuisine, something I had dabbled in but never went full throttle with learning and familiarizing myself with.

"You're late!" The words that no one wants to hear their first day on the job. And to think that I actually left my house an hour early because I wanted to impress my new boss. Tardiness was not part of the agenda. It was not my ideal first day on the job.

When I left the house, I was confident and excited about my new opportunity. However, I did not anticipate there being a shortage of parking. I mean, there was nowhere to park! I was amazed at how there was not a spot in the parking garage or community parking available. After driving around in a circle for over thirty minutes, I spotted an open parking space. *Thank you, Jesus!* I quickly parked my car and made my way to the restaurant.

Once I arrived and clocked in, I didn't think being three minutes late would be a big deal, but to my surprise, it was. From that moment on, my new chef reminded me that I was in his kitchen and nobody is ever late. Before arriving at my new place of employment, I had reached a place in my career where I felt as if I were exchanging my time for money. I found myself in a settling place, and being the person I am, this was not the mental and emotional space I needed to be in.

Everything about my culinary experience was intentional. Success is intentional. No one wakes up without ever putting in an ounce of work and is able to achieve their dreams. I in no way, form, or fashion was afraid of putting in the work. I am the son of a man who modeled hard work before me every day. And because of that, along with his love, support, and words of wisdom, I knew settling would never be an option for me.

I can recall driving into work at the resort, and as soon as I walked in, I would mentally shut down. After three years there, I viewed my time and experience there as an academic institution. I was there to learn, improve my skills and knowledge of cooking. Don't get me wrong, I met some amazing people over that course of time, but I knew it was time for me to reposition myself. I needed and wanted to know and learn more. I felt as if I was no longer being challenged, and I knew if I was going successful in the industry, I needed to explore more options. A "repositioning" was exactly what I needed.

I heard a lot about a sushi chef from Hawaii that had an amazing talent for East Asian cuisine, but I also heard he was a talented teacher, which I needed more than I realized. I did my research and quickly saw I could learn a lot from this chef.

When I applied for the job, I was interviewed by the sous chef, which surprised me. Although he was next in command, I found it odd that he had taken the lead in the interviewing process. I thought the executive chef would have taken the lead, but instead, he sat back and played a more supportive role to his sous chef.

The Love Languages of Food

The verbal portion of my interview went over pretty well. Part two of the interview process required me to prepare three separate items for tasting. The chef would use these items to determine if I was worthy enough to join the brigade. Keep in mind I had zero experience in Asian cuisine. Traditionally, I prepared what I believed they wanted and/or expected of me.

I was asked to make a salad, an appetizer, and an entree. The entire presentation took about forty-five minutes. I prepared Ahi Tuna Tostadas with Spicy Mayo, A Miso Ginger Salad with Soy Marinated Tomatoes, and a Beer Marinated Asian Flank Steak with Charred Bok Choy in a sweet Soy Reduction.

First up, the sous chef. "It's pretty good." On the other hand, the executive chef complimented the flavor profile of my dishes but felt that my execution and thoughtfulness needed a little work. And if that was not enough, he also added that overall, he expected more creativity and less tradition!

Of course, I didn't take it personally. I figured I could dwell on what he did not like and allow it to throw me off my game, or I could take the critique at face value, hold my head up and do what I had come to do - learn.

Ultimately I got hired on the spot with the understanding that I would be in an interesting spot. The chef saw my passion and potential. He told me that I would be held at a different level of responsibility and criticism because of it.

My first thirty days on the job, he was on my ass! I had heard executive chefs rant about how they ran a tight ship, but what I was experiencing was more than I ever experienced or expected. All day every day, he was right there on top of me. I started working at what they would call the "cold" station, also known as the salad station, which is the easiest station in most kitchens. Still, he was on my ass all day every day.

However, on one particular evening, I was prepping my station for dinner service. He walked up to me and asked what I was doing. I thought it was obvious. I had a large pan beside me filled with vegetables that were cut and prepared for the evening. He then grabbed the entire pan and tossed the vegetables in the trash.

We were thirty minutes away from dinner service, and my station was not prepped. At first, all I could think about was the amount of food-cost wasted, but I asked, "What was wrong with them?" He uttered that my knife skills and mastery needed some work. A lot of food was wasted, but I understood an inch too small or an inch too big was a great deal to him. This chef was serious about precision and demanded perfection.

Honestly, I had never seen anything like it. This chef was intense! I was so used to trusting my own judgment and taking mental notes, but my mental notes were no match for this chef. It was his way or the highway. And if you were wondering – yes, I made it past ninety days.

After three months, I had moved up from the cold station to the wok station. And in my opinion, it was the hardest station. The wok station was very hot and fast-paced. Proficiency and speed were a MUST! Once I had fully developed in the wok area, I requested to be trained on sushi. The executive chef did not respond with a simple yes or no. Instead, he said, "A couple of months ago, you could not cut a carrot properly, but now you want to prepare sushi with my name on it?"

He shared how he had spent two years learning to cut vegetables properly, and another two years learning to prepare rice yada, yada, yada. More importantly, he spoke of the years he had spent learning to cut fish and the additional years he committed to proficiency and mastery. He told me that I was not worthy of the time it would take to train me. Remember, the only reason I had chosen to work under him was to become proficient in sushi and East Asian cuisine. Needless to say, his response didn't stop me from working.

I showed up every day and learned all that I could learn. After his long speech, followed by a "no!" I became motivated by his "no." I decided to take matters into my own hands.

Every evening after I completed my job for the evening, I would ask other sushi chefs in the restaurant for prep jobs. I was cutting vegetables, measuring out ingredients for sticky rice, hell… getting them a cup of water. Anything that could inch me closer to learning what he told me I couldn't, I did.

I would stay past my shift to assist the sushi chefs with last-minute prepping and cleaning just to be around them. I took advantage of every opportunity to pick their brains, ask questions, and once again be a sponge. At this point, my competitive nature kicked in, and I was definitely on a mission. Whenever the executive chef wasn't around, I would watch closely as they prepared rice every evening. My mental note pad was filling up fast. I dedicated my breaks to assisting and learning from the other sushi chefs. Then, I would go home and practice preparing rice, cutting veggies, and perfecting the cuts of each fish.

Soon after, I invited friends over to taste my sushi creations. They were my sushi guinea pigs. From there, I began hosting sushi events. People would come out and walk away completely satisfied with their experience. When I saw the faces of others enjoying sushi that I prepared, it made my heart smile, especially when people stated that my sushi was just as good as, if not better than, the chef that told me I wasn't going to be ready until I was damn near thirty to even touch sushi.

Talk about VALIDATION!

Chef Manning's Orange Chicken
Inspired by *Love Language 4*

During my time learning about Asian food, I made Asian dishes every chance I could. I really wanted to immerse myself in the cuisine, so it literally became a part of my life. This is one of my favorite recipes that I developed from that time.

Let's be real! Who doesn't love orange chicken? Okay, so it's not the most authentic, but it's definitely delicious. It's the perfect go-to when you want those Asian flavors combined with your favorite vegetables and a bowl of steamed jasmine rice.

The Sauce
3 oranges, juiced and zested
1/3 cup of sugar
6 tablespoons of sesame oil
2 tablespoons of white vinegar
5 tablespoons of soy sauce
3 cups of mushroom broth
8 tablespoons of ginger garlic

The Batter
1 cup of cornstarch
3 eggs
1 cup of water
Mix all ingredients and add salt

The Elements
6 chicken breasts, thinly sliced
2 teaspoons of garlic
2 teaspoons of ginger
2 teaspoons of soy sauce
1 bunch of green onions, chopped
1 teaspoon of brown sugar

Take Action

1. Marinate chicken in chopped garlic, chopped ginger, soy sauce, chopped green onions, and brown sugar for two hours.
2. Dip the cut chicken breasts into batter and fry at 350°F for 5-7 minutes.
3. Toss in orange sauce while hot.

Love Language 5
Cuisine & Culture

Cuisine is what connects the human race with food. Whether it be soul food, East Asian, or Indian, each cuisine has certain staple dishes that are must-haves! It's even better when these staples are experienced in their region. Sushi in Japan, Pasta in Italy, or even Fish & Chips in England. Having these specialties will make you want to travel the world just for food. You might gain some weight along the way, but it will be happy weight.

"We may not always admit it, but we all have a cuisine that we prefer; it's very similar to having a spirit animal or a best friend. My personal favorite is East Asian cuisine. This is probably because of what I had to endure to get my training for the cuisine. Once I learned the history of the culture, I developed a true appreciation for it."

-Chef Terrell Manning

No matter what region you visit, you will always notice a distinct difference in the food and develop an appreciation for certain dishes, textures, and flavor profiles. In fact, food is considered to be a universal form of communication. We may not all speak the same languages, but we all love food. Not just any food, but good food that speaks to our soul, food that embodies our culture and our everyday lives.

Imagine the love somebody feels when a meal is being prepared for them that they've never tasted or experienced before. Envision the look on someone's face when served one of their favorite meals prepared by a loved one…

As a kid, I enjoyed seeing the smile on my mother's face as she and my father dressed up for date night. My mother could count on my father taking her to one of her favorite restaurants, which always made my mom happy. It is that same joy and happiness that pulled me into the creative world of culinary, knowing that people are excited to come into my restaurant to have an amazing dining experience from dishes that I've put my heart and soul into perfecting.

After nearly two years of developing my skills to perfect the art of sushi, I began to wonder what else could I learn and accomplish on my own. After receiving validation from my chefs, guests, critics, peers, friends, and family, I knew my next move would be to authenticate my chef experience by exploring more!

The Love Languages of Food

The fact that food is a unifier across cultures, and I am a culturally diverse person, I was ready to advance my all-around skill, increase my knowledge, and develop globally in the culinary industry. I desired to reach the pinnacle of my profession. I knew and understood the "why" of what I was going after. I was in a place where not only was I excited about learning and evolving as a chef, but I discovered that my in-depth passion and zeal for cooking had created its own love language.

I found it all to be interesting that at the age of twenty-one, I had excelled and worked with some of the best chefs from all over the world and was now establishing myself as a multifaceted chef that could work in practically any kitchen environment and could cook almost any cuisine. For me, advancement always had meaning and purpose, but now it was also personal. I had something to prove to myself!

As a chef, I did not want to build a predictable career. I knew that I would get better every day and become a force to be reckoned with in the culinary industry. I am an envelope pusher by nature. I respect rules and authority, but I also believe that bending and breaking them to improve the nature of a craft is the very thing that leads to personal greatness. I will never settle!

I began as a boy with a special interest in cooking. I was now a young man turned chef! I figured if, for some reason, God called me home at any moment, I wanted to take my last breath knowing I did everything I could to perfect my craft. Some may say that it's a little dramatic, but nothing is more dramatic than a person with passion and purpose.

Truth be told, I overdo everything! I give every area of my craft 110%. If I had to add up the number of hours and days that I spend self-educating and training, I would pass out trying to count them all. One of the most important things about passion-filled and purpose-driven individuals is the enjoyment of the application.

Every station I ever worked, I gave my all. Every chef I worked under, I learned something new and different from them. Every dish I cooked, I cooked it like it was my last. There was no job too small and no job too big. I was fully committed!

Being an experienced chef, I could work in any kitchen and not have to begin at the bottom. The countless hours of self-educating and training led me to this point. I'm now fluent in a multitude of cuisines. I believe it's important when learning cultural cuisines to learn from an individual of the culture who prepares, serves, and eats their cultural dishes regularly. This doesn't always mean a chef; it could be a friend, spouse, grandmother, whoever…

By expanding my cultural horizons, I knew a trip around the globe would one day happen, but for now, I needed to seek out locals that I could learn from about their particular culture, food, and traditions. My go-getter mentality was fully on display. For instance, I have a good deal of friends that are from various parts of the Caribbean islands. I noticed that each island prepared jerk chicken distinctively different. I honed in on each island's flavor profile, taste, and texture, asked for recipes from each friend and or family member, and practiced each recipe at home until I mastered each jerk chicken recipe to a T. I quickly discovered that everybody loves a lot of the same foods, they just enjoy it differently.

I had learned so much that I began sharing my knowledge with others in the industry and bringing light and inspiration to having more culturally diverse menus and ingredients. People in the industry began seeking me out to teach them what I had learned. The knowledge that I would share was not limited to only chefs. Clients also sought out my knowledge. One of the most rewarding experiences for a chef is the response we receive when others sing praises of living up to what you promise.

Chef Manning's Creole Jambalaya
Inspired by *Love Language 5*

Each ingredient in this dish plays a very distinctive role in the flavor profile and are each equally important to the result of this amazing jambalaya. I remember driving up to Louisiana to visit a couple of my cousins. Of course, I wanted to see them and have a good time, but I knew there would be some wonderful Louisiana cuisine, and I wanted to learn as much as I could about the food they cooked. To this day, this is one of my favorite recipes and is so easy to make.

The Elements

2 diced onions
2 red peppers
2 green peppers
1 celery cut on a bias
2 shredded carrots
4 crushed or smashed tomatoes
1 tablespoon of honey
1 cup of andouille sausage, diced
¾ pound of ground pork or sausage
1 pound of shrimp, peeled & deveined
¼ pound of lump crab
¼ pound of lobster, chopped
Salt, pepper, and cayenne pepper for taste

Take Action

1. Cook vegetables on a medium-high heat with olive oil.
2. Sweat down ingredients in ¼ cup of Louisiana Hot Sauce until translucent; add salt and pepper to taste.
3. Begin to cook the rice by heating a pot of water. Add salt to the water so that the water will boil faster. It will also season the water.
4. Cook rice until softened to a desirable texture.

5. By this time, the vegetables should be cooked enough to where you can add in your andouille sausage and ground sausage and season with salt, pepper, and cayenne pepper.
6. Once the rice is cooked, add it into the mixture, stir and mix in.
7. After 5 minutes, toss in the peeled and deveined shrimp and jumbo lump crab. Mix well.
8. After 15 minutes, taste a forkful with all proteins to ensure proteins are cooked thoroughly and seasoned to perfection.

Love Language 6
Validation & Confirmation

"No true artist really needs validation from other people, but it's great to have. Not just from friends or family but also people who don't give a shit about hurting your feelings, just a good solid overall critique. Receiving the good critiques and compliments can really boost one's confidence and propel them to want to advance their career and hone in on what they are already good at. It forces them to focus on improving what they aren't good at while also receiving confirmation about their current cooking abilities."

-Chef Terrell Manning

One of the greatest gifts I have ever received was from guests after experiencing my famous tomato bruschetta. I can recall using the most beautiful Sonoma County Roma tomatoes, finely chopped garlic, a very rich extra virgin olive oil, roasted red peppers, fresh basil, mint leaves, and a reduced balsamic vinegar. Just witnessing how intrigued they were as I shared details of the back history of the dish and how I got the inspiration to prepare the dish was exhilarating. To be truthful, nothing makes me feel happier than seeing the look of satisfaction on the faces of my guests.

Yes, I'm a chef, but I put a lot more into what I do and offer. Most people don't understand the depth of what is required of a chef. The behind-the-scenes parts of this industry are far more work than many expect or understand it to be. Chefs are required to be self-motivating, fast learners, quick listeners, and timely executers. Every minute and hour in a kitchen is extremely crucial; there's always time to learn, create, prep, clean, catch up on inventory, etc. There is no downtime. It's go, go, go from the minute your nonslip shoes hit the kitchen floor.

When our guests are happy, we are happy and not a minute before. We want their validation and confirmation of a meal well prepared. Their validation is important to the overall experience. A chef needs the validation of the customer to ensure that the kitchen is in a smooth flow. From the peeling and slicing of vegetables down to the minute we plate the food, our main goal is to present our personal best on every plate we serve; it is our signature of approval.

It wasn't until I realized the importance of food from a consumer standpoint that I broke free from cooking at an introvert level. Before I learned how to properly create menus based on seasonal trends and fresh, innovative ingredients, I would stick to the basic things that I knew and would rarely venture out for new experiences.

As I became more experienced, I began listening to what my clients wanted or fancied. I would add certain popular components, but of course, I tweaked it to add my own spin.

I have found that it is important for chefs to make an authentic connection with consumers. By doing so, trust is developed, which could lead to repeat clients, more business, and more money, but overall, a great dining experience. Offering customers a personalized experience helps chefs to connect on a more intimate and emotional level. You never want to dismiss attention to detail. Consumers love details, and any real chef thrives off of details. More details mean you put in more work. It means you spent time studying and perfecting, and most importantly, it means you know what you're talking about.

I experienced it firsthand, as people would recognize me and share how they are fans of my work. They often shared how they had become trusting of my brand, my abilities, as well as my creative artistry. That level of validation is always appreciated. I put in a lot of time to achieve that level of respect from guests, peers, colleagues, and other chefs.

Interestingly, I can recall wanting to impress this one chef. He was very strict and very particular about the *soup du jour* or soup of the day. However, that's nothing new. All chefs have that one thing they're overly aware of, and his was soup du jour. No matter how much I tried to impress him, he never acknowledged it. It was as if I were invisible. And if you have learned anything about me from reading my book, I am not okay with being invisible. He was a well-respected chef in the industry. I most certainly respected him, and I desired to be respected by him.

I went to sleep one night after a long and busy dinner service. I remember having a dream about this fantastic tomato bisque. In the dream, the chef complimented the soup and my enthusiasm on making it while knowing how particular he was.

The next day, I got to work super early with a recipe written out from everything I remembered in the dream. The recipe would soon earn me the respect of being seen and the validation I was seeking. I knew exactly how I wanted the texture of the bisque. I knew the color that I wanted it to have, and I knew how it should taste. I envisioned it over and over the night before. As soon as I walked into work, I vigorously began working.

One of the other chefs noticed and walked over to inquire. I responded by sharing that I was preparing a special soup for the evening. He then smiled, and as he walked away, he wished me luck. They all knew how protective the executive chef was about his soups. Soup was his signature dish.

To all of my colleagues, I was treading in dangerous territory, and if it were not better than great, it could cost me my position in his kitchen. As the executive chef walked in, he too asked what I was doing. I replied, "Trying to impress you." He gave me a very intense stare, and as he turned to walk away, he looked back at me and said, "It better be fucking good." This only added to my nervousness, but the edge forced me to create perfection. I felt pressure to succeed. It was a small task, but, at that moment, it felt like everything was on the line. Everything had to be perfect.

Once it was ready, I offered everyone in the kitchen a taste test. They each said it was perfect and delicious. I knew without a shadow of a doubt that it was "fucking good!" I had found a way to become visible and earn his respect. The moment of truth had arrived, and I was confident that I had nailed it.

As the chef journeyed over to where the soup was with a spoon in hand, he first smelled it. The aromatics were good! He then stirred it, and the texture was good! And lastly, he tasted it. If I had to describe it, it was as if we were all in a movie. Everything slowed down to almost a sudden stop as the chef tasted my soup.

As the spoon entered his mouth, everyone looked on quietly, including me. "Really great soup, bud," were the words he uttered out of his mouth. My heart felt as if it had dropped out of my chest. The chef who never wanted to give me credit for anything validated me in front of everyone, and it felt really amazing.

Chef Manning's Bread Pudding & Rum Sauce

Inspired by *Love Language 6*

    I started working on this recipe when the chef, who was a hard nose about soups, told me that he loves a great bread pudding. I decided to try my winning hand and came up with this incredibly delicious and moist bread pudding.

The Elements

3 loaves of bread
6 eggs, separated
12 tablespoons of butter, melted
3 ¾ cups of brown sugar
4 teaspoons of cinnamon
4 teaspoons of vanilla
1 double boiler
1 cup of raisins
1 cup of chocolate chips
1 ¼ cups of sugar
3 ¼ cups of heavy cream
5 oz of Bacardi Gold Rum

The Cremé

1. Start by placing heavy cream on low heat.
2. Add in rum and egg whites. Wisk thoroughly
3. After two minutes, add sugar and whisk until thickened.

Take Action

1. Dice bread loaves into small parts.
2. Heat double boiler to medium heat.
3. Add all of the melted butter into the double boiler.
4. Fold egg yolks into the butter gradually.
5. Whisk moderately and try not to create bubbles.

6. Add in brown sugar, cinnamon, and vanilla flavoring.
7. After 3 minutes of whisking, add in raisins and chocolate chips
8. Once thoroughly whisked, add mixture to the diced bread and stir until fully coated and place in a baking pan.
9. Bake for 40 minutes at 360°F; poke with a toothpick to check doneness.

Love Language 7
Friendship & Camaraderie

"One of the most overshadowed things about cooking with others is the endless amounts of fun and enjoyment you can receive from it. I often think about the fantastic times I've had with family and friends in the kitchen and the relationships I've developed with random strangers. I wouldn't trade those moments for anything in the world."

-Chef Terrell Manning

Some of the best moments of my life were spent with people I will never see again. I have had amazing experiences that I never wanted to end. In those moments, it seemed as if it was me and them against the world! And there was never a time that we did not rise to the occasion. We all loved everything about the kitchen equally. The camaraderie built between co-workers, the sound of sizzling pans, the artistry of the plates, the arguments, and shoving matches on the line — nothing short of amazing!

The beauty of it all gives off a high that keeps me coming back for more. Everyone who has experienced

The Love Languages of Food

the world of culinary and has lived to talk about it will revisit the memories repeatedly. There's a very different level of excitement and energy associated with it. You're showing up to work with excitement. You're prepping with excitement, and of course, you're cooking with excitement. I love everything there is to love about the environment. As I stated before, the experience is nothing short of a movie!

My passion for food and cooking, along with my eagerness to enhance and improve, is what drives me. I am what some would call a cooking enthusiast! Cooking, eating, and enjoying great company is the thing that brings us all together, be it a private meal, a social outing at your favorite restaurant, or a meal prepared at home in your kitchen. All of these options offer a unique experience that opens the doors to the beautiful world of culinary.

Imagine you and a group of people sitting at a table enjoying a fabulous meal together. Everyone has the same meal, but each experience is different. That is the love language of food. As a cooking and food enthusiast, I always ask, "Who is the consumer? What is it that they want? Where are the opportunities for me to try something new, to create and deliver an unexpected experience?"

Outside of my industry, I experienced many the same enjoyments preparing special meals for special occasions, for some very special people all in the comfort of my home. I must admit, the same zeal and excitement I get from cooking in a professional kitchen is equivalent to me cooking at home in my kitchen. I would say the only difference is that everyone creates the experience that they prefer at home. You select your guest, decide on the menu, choose the wine selections, and confirm the entertainment. You have total control of your in-home culinary experience.

Memories such as these remind me of the true meaning of "cooking from the heart." If you aren't cooking from the heart, you shouldn't be cooking at all.

If someone were to ask me why I do what I do, my answer would be simple. I do it because it fuels me, it excites me, it challenges me, and it humbles me. Everything about the culinary industry pushes me to become a better chef, a better man, and a better culinary artist. I apply the same work ethic and values in a professional kitchen in my personal kitchen. There's a lot of hard work that goes into preparing every salad, appetizer, dessert, and entrée that's served. Every detail of what consumers experience is premeditated.

It's all about what you cannot see, all the hard work that happens behind the scenes. Chefs work tirelessly! Cooking is a way of LIFE. Cooking consumes our lives. To be the kind of chef that is respected and acknowledged, it requires dedication and a level of commitment that many will never understand.

For example, I have visited farms to learn about the animals and their diets and living conditions before deciding if the meat is fit for the consumer. I am also an advocate for tasting vegetables and fruit right there in their natural habitat where they are grown. However, one of my personal favorites is meeting the fisherman who caught the fresh catch of the day.

You have to be confident in who you are and what you're doing. Wolfgang Puck said it best; "A chef is a mixture maybe of artistry and craft. You have to learn the craft really to get there."

The Love Languages of Food

Chef Manning's Butter Cookies Recipe
Inspired by *Love Language 7*

Nothing, absolutely nothing brings people together like the smell of butter cookies fresh out of the oven! Love Language 7 is all about bringing people together and enjoying beautiful memories like eating a warm butter cookie with friends. It might sound corny, but hey! Sometimes corny times are the best of times.

I stumbled upon this recipe because my mother would make some similar cookies that were not quite butter cookies. So, I decided to toy around with it, and ever since then, these amazing treats have been a staple.

The Elements
1 cup of butter, softened
2/3 cup of powdered sugar, sifted
½ teaspoon of vanilla extract
½ teaspoon of butter extract
1/3 cup of sifted corn starch
¼ teaspoon of salt

Take Action
1. Soften 1 cup of butter.
2. Place 2/3 cup of sifted powdered sugar on top of softened butter.
3. Mix in stick mixer until light and fluffy.
4. Add in ½ teaspoon of vanilla extract and ½ teaspoon of butter extract; beat until incorporated.
5. Add in 1 1/2 cups plus 1 additional tablespoon of sifted All Purpose flour.
6. Add in 1/3 cup of sifted corn starch.
7. Add to mix in two small batches.
8. Mix in the first half and after combined, fold in the second half.

9. Mix until combined.
10. Add in ¼ teaspoon of salt.
11. Transfer to a piping bag.
12. Pipe out rosettes.
13. Refrigerate for 20-30 minutes.
14. Bake at 340°F for 12-15 minutes.
15. Allow to cool completely.

About Chef Manning

Terrell Manning is a highly-skilled private chef and founder of Manning Catering and Healthy Eatz Delivery. Chef Manning's knowledge of culinary arts has expanded his business brand and has been shared with chefs worldwide.

As a culinary entrepreneur, Terrell is committed to teaching future chefs the bigger and powerful vision of the demanding culinary industry to ensure that he provides others with the tools he was not equipped with before starting his career.

For catering inquiries, please visit chefterrellmanning.com

www.ingramcontent.com/pod-product-compliance
Lightning Source LLC
Chambersburg PA
CBHW041807160426
43209CB00015B/1720